Forget Me Not

Shelby L. Michalek

Collaborator

Megan Hedglen

Copyright © 2023 Shelby L. Michalek

All rights reserved.

ISBN: 9798871652558

PROFESSIONAL ACKNOWLEDGEMENTS

Megan Hedglen

Thank you for your commitment and desire to contribute to this story. Your guidance and professional knowledge gave this book the words that are *so* necessary for anyone struggling to hear.

Thank you, thank you, thank you.

Megan Hedglen (formerly Megan McHugh), co-founder of The Therapy Collective, is a licensed professional counselor (LPC) and is credentialed by the National Board of Certified Counselors as a National Certified Counselor (NCC). Areas of interest for Megan include working to treat depression and those struggling with anxiety and panic disorders. Wellness strategies and Cognitive Behavioral approaches are cornerstones of treatment. Megan also enjoys working with clients who have previously struggled in finding the "right therapist" and believes in personal approaches in treatment. Megan has obtained a Master's degree in counseling (M.Ed.), a Master's degree in elementary education (M.Ed.), as well as an undergraduate degree in Psychology (BA) from California University of Pennsylvania.

Outside of the office, Megan is a wife and mother of two boys. Megan enjoys the outdoors, anything funny, and drinking too much coffee.

More information about The Therapy Collective can be found at: thetherapycollective.net

CONTENTS

Preface: Why I Wrote This   Pg.5

1. My Story   Pg. 7
2. Hang On   Pg. 25
3. Navigating the Storm   Pg. 32
4. Hard Truths   Pg. 43
5. Your Brain and Grief   Pg. 53
6. No Rain No Flowers   Pg. 77
7. Moving Forward for Them   Pg. 81
8. Epilogue: Genetics   Pg. 85

Dedication   Pg. 96

WHY I WROTE THIS BOOK

I wrote this for anyone who's had to know sorrow, regardless of the type of loss. I wrote about infant loss because it's what I know, but grief is universal.

I know you don't feel like you have time to continue feeling how you do; but time, though it can move very slowly, does in fact heal. I'm careful to not say "heal all," because it can't and won't. But, I guarantee you that if you hang on, life will become less painful - and dare I say, even enjoyable again. We are so much more resilient than we think we are.

I wanted a way forward in this time of extreme heartache. I wanted to regain my footing, and eventually, I did. I wrote this to help anyone who's looking for that lifeline like I was. I wrote this as a reminder that moving forward doesn't mean forgetting.

In searching for self-help resources, I found that much of the available material was faith based, with the focus being on my baby in heaven, and how our love transcends to the other side. Now, I would love my son to be up in the sky, enjoying the afterlife to the fullest extent. However, in all honesty, I struggle with that belief. It's much easier for us to consider the outcome of someone who passes away to be up there, better off, than to face the scary idea that maybe our loved one simply no longer exists on any plane. That possibility is sometimes too much to wrap our heads around when we are already drowning in grief and shock.

Now I'm not entirely dismissing the idea of Heaven, I'm simply saying I don't know what I don't know. Losing a loved one shakes your faith. Losing a baby shatters it to pieces.

So, until I can speak to someone on the other side, I need comfort here. We need human love and connection. When my spiritual faith was gone, faith in humanity is what saved me. In writing this I'm trying to pay that forward.

My Story

"Motherhood: The only place you can experience Heaven and Hell at the same time."
- Anonymous

This story is going to go into some medical details. Some of which may not make sense just yet, but in order to give a full picture of everything, I need to include them; they are important, I promise. All stories have context. In stories of loss, the death is the event that strikes you with grief - but the cumulative list of traumas surrounding that death often also need healing from.

I became pregnant for the first time when I was twenty-eight years old. After a few years of marriage, continuing down the track of a "typical" life, my husband and I felt it was time to start a family. And what do you know, within the first few months of trying, there it was: the stick showing the famous two pink lines. None of the females in my family had ever had any fertility or genetic issues that I knew of, so I thought that it would be an easy breezy nine months. How lucky was I?

I had an ultrasound at nine weeks to confirm the pregnancy. As I laid on the table, silence swelled within the room that was just full of happy, chatty small talk. I could feel the instantaneous shift of the energy, and dread raced through me. The ultrasound tech had a hard time making eye contact and quietly relayed the finding. The pregnancy was no longer viable. I was classified as having a missed miscarriage, since my body showed no physical symptoms of the loss. To say I felt shocked was an understatement. This was the first of many times to come when I would feel a trap door open beneath me. I was now a statistic that's only heard about. This loss was hard and I was undeniably heartbroken. But I was able to comprehend that this is harsh, but common outcome. Not wanting to sit and lick my wounds, I quickly decided to try again.

I was pregnant again mere months later. This time around I was optimistic but more cautious. I opted to have genetic testing - not because we carried a family history of any genetic conditions, but because it was a way to get an ultrasound faster. I was concerned with just scheduling an appointment to make sure the baby was okay. My anxiety palpable, I laid, waiting for any signal of good information. There it was – a strong heartbeat. Relief is an understatement. This was it; baby was okay. I called my husband while still laying on the ultrasound table as soon as the tech left to give him the happy news. However, the tech didn't return, instead in came a doctor who took her place. He sat down and took over, feverishly clicking and intensely analyzing the screen. Something was clearly wrong. His body language and flat tone of voice in trying to initiate small talk said it all. I was so confused, the heartbeat was clearly there, I was watching it flickering on screen – so what else would be a cause of concern? After a few agonizing minutes, I finally worked up the courage, "Is everything okay?" I choked out, even though I didn't want his answer. He eventually turned to me and said in a very matter of fact manner that my baby had an anatomy marker that usually indicates a birth defect. *Trap door opens.*

In the following days, I had a procedure done to get a more detailed look at the baby's genetics. The wait for the results was grueling. I was terrified to take that call from the genetic counselor. When it came, I reluctantly answered, bracing for impact. But the impact didn't come. Everything had tested normal; our baby was genetically healthy. Tears ran down my face as the counselor explained the results. I felt so unbelievably grateful, though I knew we weren't entirely out of the woods just yet. We proceeded with caution, advised by the doctors and genetic counselor that the marker could also indicate a heart condition that wouldn't be detectable or diagnosable until week twenty, mid-way through the pregnancy. They didn't know and couldn't even speculate to what severity it would impact the baby, if at all. We took the good news as that and put that final hurdle in the back of our minds for the time being.

Spring evolved into summer. We spent the time planning for our growing family. As my bump continued to grow and the kicks became stronger so did our optimism and confidence that everything would be okay.

Week twenty was around the corner, and all our nerves were on edge. It was time for the fetal echocardiogram, a specialized ultrasound test used to evaluate the position, size, structure, function, and rhythm of the baby's heart. I laid on the exam table with clenched fists, barely breathing, anticipating the news we were long awaiting. Finally, he spoke, "Perfect." Everything looked great! The heart looked healthy and normal. Of all the outcomes I ran through my head in the months previously this was obviously the absolute best-case scenario, it didn't even feel real. Our follow up appointment with the genetic counselor was cancelled, she met us in the waiting room and with a big smile, "looks like baby was just giving us a scare!" she beamed as she waved us off. We walked, *maybe even skipped* of the hospital in awe of how lucky we were. Having that confirmation, we ripped open the envelope containing the baby's gender. We were having a boy! Our hearts couldn't have been any fuller. It was time to celebrate.

I had a few months of relief and excitement for the future. I fully embraced my pregnancy. After the initial tumultuous months, I felt so lucky to still have him with me. I was finally able to partake in the fun parts of expecting. I will always be grateful for this time. Ignorance is bliss, after all.

At my thirty-two-week check- up, I expressed that over the weekend the baby's movements had slowed a bit. I was more so making casual conversation, I truly didn't think too much of it. Just to be safe, the doctor hooked me up to a nonstress test (*aptly named*), and relayed that the baby's heartrate classified as non-reactive, meaning it didn't match up to his physical movements as it should. This finding was the start of what would become a month-long saga of living in and out of the hospital. All doctors could tell me was that there may be something wrong, or there may be nothing wrong, the problem could be me, or it could be him - I wouldn't know any real answers until I gave birth. *Good stuff. Very comforting.* How did we find ourselves here again? And with such continued ambiguity? I pressed for answers about how or what could be happening? What were these doctors theorizing could be wrong? I did all the things, passed all the tests, he was healthy? I could not get a straight answer. Weeks thirty-two to thirty-seven consisted of ultrasounds every few days, along with overnight stays and monitoring. Despite all the chaos, uncertainty, and frustrations, I could not wait to meet our baby boy. He was my little guy, and I loved him so much already. I just needed him to be born so I could end this nightmare pregnancy and hold him in my arms. I kept trying to convince myself this will just be a crazy story we would reflect on and tell him someday in his future. *Convince* being a key word, in all honesty I had no idea what our future held in these weeks. I was nervous enough about becoming a mom in general. My life was about to change dramatically regardless, but now I had to attempt to prepare well beyond that.

Doctors agreed to induce me early, and of all days, on my thirtieth birthday. I started my induction at 12:00 p.m. on November 4th, 2021. This was the beginning of what turned into a strenuous thirty-two-hour labor, ending in a Cesarean delivery. Through complete distortion, I remember them pulling my baby out and calling the time - 12:32 a.m. on November 6th, 2021, Hank Ryan Michalek entered this world.

I was not fully there, I was actually *barely* there when I eventually gave birth. My brain couldn't on the surface comprehend what was happening or why they took my son from me immediately. Like a lot of other things, my delivery wasn't fair. I should never have gone that long attempting a vaginal birth when doctors knew something was most likely wrong with my baby - even more so than what they had let on, I found out later. In retrospect, though, had I been fully coherent and observant, it would have panicked when he was taken immediately. My state of delirium most likely saved me from some shock.

I couldn't meet my son until about 4:00 a.m. that morning. I was so disoriented, I remember knowing that he was my baby, but couldn't register anything else. His tiny body had wired hooked up everywhere. He was intubated, but I was unable to grasp exactly what that meant. It took everything in me just to stay conscious - I couldn't even string a sentence together. I had absolutely no wherewithal to comprehend the severity of the situation.

Next thing I know it was morning. They rolled him beside me in an incubator and informed me he was going via ambulance to Children's Hospital. I still can't recall what I was thinking in these moments. I don't even remember saying goodbye to him. Off he went with my husband while I stayed at my delivery hospital to recover. I wasn't allowed to leave until the minimum recovery time was up and I was cleared. I was scared, alone, and in pain. I wouldn't accept medication because I had to detox from my delivery. I didn't know what was going on, but I knew I had to get clear headed so I could face it. I had to pull myself together so I could leave and be his mom. I had grown this little human, given birth to him, and had yet to even touch him. I was alone, surrounded by crying babies on the maternity floor, while my mind was consumed with how distressed he also was. I had to put my faith in strangers to care and comfort him. An intense ache of longing ran through me. Hank and I were separated when we needed each other most.

After two days, I was released.

When I was reunited with Hank, it didn't feel like he was mine. I had to ask permission to hold him for the first time. I couldn't squeeze him against my chest without the risk of knocking his wires and tube loose, which would have serious effects on his breathing. It was torture not to be able to just scoop my baby in my arms and comfort him the way nature wants and humans need.

I never wanted to cause suffering to anything in this world; but here I was, watching my very own baby struggle to survive before my very eyes. I felt guilty I made him, and that he was now so helpless and stuck in this condition. Doctors or experts can say whatever they want about how much he didn't yet understand, but he was uncomfortable, scared, and suffering.

We were approached by palliative care early on to test the waters of our beliefs and thoughts. As you can imagine, the discussion is something impossible to prepare for. I was so confused how we'd gotten to where we were? Yes, I understood that I hadn't had the smoothest pregnancy. But never once did I consider that if I made it to him being born, he wouldn't come home with me. I mean we live in a time of modern medicine. How could this be unfixable? How was there no potential cure? Before we received Hank's official diagnosis, I was very forthright in sharing that I was not going to sentence my child to lying in a hospital bed, for the duration of what would be an extremely short, hard life, all just to lessen my own pain. These early conversations were surreal and difficult, and related to what we thought as an unlikely scenario.

We never imagined we would have to actually live through it.

Hank's breathing tube was removed in one of the earlier days to evaluate his capability to breathe on his own. We watched helplessly as his blood oxygen plummeted to 14 percent. To give some context, for a newborn, that number should remain around 90-100 percent. Anything below is of concern. Hank's doctor and nurses flooded into the room. I was watching him die before my eyes, and all I could do was run into the bathroom and fall on the floor, sobbing. I needed nothing more than for him to recover in those moments, and he somehow did. He was able to be re-intubated in time and stabilized. This outcome verified what everyone had been dreading; Hank couldn't, and would never be able, keep himself alive without medical intervention.

There is a lot more I could say about this time, and the darkness that came with it, but you can use your imagination. Over the course of the following days, it was discovered that my son had type 0/1 SMA. Spinal Muscular Atrophy (SMA) is a progressive neurodegenerative disease that affects the motor nerve cells in the spinal cord and impacts the muscles, causing them to atrophy. Hank didn't have the muscle tone to move or to breathe on his own. With his severe case, Hank was never going to live a life free of heavy medical equipment. Hank was never going to leave the hospital.

What was happening didn't make any sense to us or to his doctors, considering I'd had genetic testing done throughout my pregnancy, SMA should have been ruled out early on, especially considering it is one of the more common genetic disorders. As I was able to unfold in the months following, it turns out my initial providers never tested blood work specific to SMA which was in fact ordered early in my first trimester. I had many blood draws in my pregnancy, assuming they were completing all the correct and ordered scripts, I mean why wouldn't they be? They're doctors after all. If any of the numerous medical professionals involved in my case would have noticed it was missed, they would have discovered by a simple blood test that I was a carrier for SMA, and then tested my husband who would have also been found to be a carrier. With probably more than twenty ultrasounds, blood samples, the involvement of genetic counselors, multiple obstetricians, and renowned high-risk doctors' supervision, it was truly baffling how something like this was overlooked. Now, our family had to pay the price.

Watching him helpless is the worst feeling I've ever felt, and it probably always will be. That feeling is what led to the hardest decision that, I would argue, any human could be forced to make. We were going to redirect his care. I hated the word "decision". I still despise it. It wasn't a decision at all; it was an inescapable verdict.

I knew that I would soon have a hard time remembering what my son looked like, his smell, how he felt, the feeling I had when his eyes would meet mine. In these moments, I was already grieving him while holding him in my arms. I had a very small window of time to wrap my head around preemptive grief. By the time I knew it was coming, I had only a few days to do my absolute best to readjust my mindset so I could enjoy the time I had left with him. I knew that I would revisit these memories with him for the rest of my life, so I did my best to pivot away from my own stress and just focus every ounce of energy I had on comforting him.

Sitting in the hospital, I would stare at his face so focused. I would try to run the life he should have had through my head – holidays, sports, going to school dances, learning things from his dad, milestone birthdays, getting married, having kids of his own. I played him all different genres of music, in the short time he had, I was trying to allow him to experience even a small fraction of what life had to offer. I was trying to sear every single moment into my mind. I wanted, and needed to remember every distinguishing feature of his. I had to absorb as much of him as humanly possible. I hope he somehow knew how much he is absolutely, fiercely, and *truly* loved.

In that time, and even now, I never really felt sorry for myself. I feel irreparably heartbroken, but I wasn't the victim - he was. I felt such intense sorrow for him. Life was unfair to him. I wished so badly we could trade places. He had no say, no choices, no opportunities. He wasn't even given a chance to experience happiness, he only knew pain. The way his life turned out was cruel, and I have to live on with that. But what I was able to give him was dignity in death. That is something not many of us get in life. Not for one day since his passing have I questioned my resolve. Not once.

That being so, after nine trying days, we held our son as he was taken off medical support and he took his last breaths. It was the first time I had ever seen his face clearly, without a tube blocking his features, and was able to finally embrace him with no interference. I'm going to make the most customary mom comment here, but he was truly the most beautiful baby I'd ever seen. The irony of the situation is not lost on me, as I was clearly seeing him for the first time, I was losing him in the same moments. On November 15th, 2021, Hank Ryan Michalek left this world.

After he passed, I handed him directly to the nurse, and told her to take him away. I didn't want to remember him lifeless. I stood up, shaking, hugged his doctor, and I thanked the nurses. I went into autopilot, I slipped my shoes and coat on, and swiftly started the walk out of the hospital.

"Surreal" is not the proper word. I'm not sure there even is one. We drove home in silence with an empty car seat sitting behind us. I remember continually looking back and just staring at it, praying this was some nightmare I was going to wake up from. Anyone who draws the incredibly short stick of leaving the hospital without their baby will say that trip is forever burned into their memory. We walked into our home, and it had never felt emptier. Despite leaving as two and coming home as two, there was a cosmic shift. We started the difficult journey of navigating life after loss.

The funeral was four days later, I did fine. It was the first time most people had seen me since their last vision of an optimistic, bumping, eager mom to be. I now looked very different. Nonetheless, I think they were probably surprised at how well I was holding up. I, myself, was surprised. You think a funeral is the most difficult part, where you should be a shell of yourself. But, considering the two weeks I had just experienced, the funeral was by far the easiest day. I think part of me was in shock. What this ended up being was a calm before the storm. I thought I was doing as well as someone in my position possibly could, but in the week following Hank's funeral, grief overtook me like a tidal wave, and I was in no way equipped to handle what was to come.

I spiraled down into a major depressive episode, compounded by extreme anxiety, postpartum hormone changes, surgical recovery, and raw grief. My mental health was absolutely obliterated, and I could not see an outcome in which I made it out the other side of this.

If I'm being completely transparent – a small part of me didn't want to get better. I knew deep down in the parts of my brain that were still rational that I would not always feel this way; but I'd seen what the world had to offer, and I didn't want any part of it. As life goes, this would not be the last time my heart would break open, and I didn't want any more pain. I felt like I was at the absolute limit of what a human could endure for a lifetime, and I couldn't handle another blow no matter when it would happen.

I knew that, even after all this pain, I still desperately wanted to be a mother. I also knew that, in order to get what I wanted, I would have to endure another pregnancy and delivery. It would be like getting in a car wreck that almost killed you, only to have to get right back into the car. It took work, patience, and time. Eventually, I was ready to try. It took me eight months to finally see those clear two lines again. This was it, somewhat of a happy ending was in sight, a sense of relief was finally in my future, and a piece of Hank was going to be back in my arms.

Everything looked great at eight weeks - strong heartbeat, perfect measuring. Seeing a life growing inside of me again was wrought with emotions. Ultrasounds had become very tolling on me, but seeing this glimmer of hope was indescribable. I knew I had a long road ahead, but we were optimistic.

At eleven weeks we went in for a procedure for genetic testing. I cried from stress on the way to the hospital, overwhelmed with stress. Even though the procedure itself is uncomfortable, I wasn't nervous about that; I'd had the same test in my last pregnancy and handled it just fine. What I was terrified of was that there wasn't going to be a heartbeat. I tried to push that ruminating thought as far away as I could, I had a lot of reasons to be concerned but that one shouldn't have been at the top of mind. As I laid down on the table to begin the procedure, silence fell over the room, an observation I had become too familiar with interpreting. The tech letting out a muffled "I'm sorry." confirming my intuition. *Trap, meet door.*

I calmly got off of the ultrasound table and walked out of the hospital in complete dissociation without speaking a word. To this day, I can still feel the internal vibrations of pure shock I felt in that moment. I had barely made it through, had brought myself back from the dead, only to have my world crash down again. I'd already learned that life wasn't fair, so this was a reminder I really did not need. That fear of my heart breaking open again came to life. And came quick.

I endured through the pain, and allowed life to teach me it's painful, yet important lessons.

And again, I survived.

As I was starting IVF, I happened to become pregnant again…

And at nine weeks, I miscarried.

And again, I survived.

I'll explain why things turned out this way later on. This story covers a lot, and there are many different parts that are important to share and bring awareness to.

But for now, let's dive into why most of you picked this book up. Let's talk about the thing no one likes to talk about; grief.

Hang On

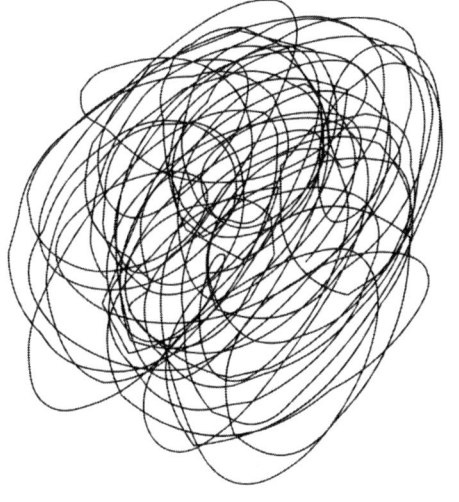

"There is hope, even when your brain tells you there isn't."
- John Green

Grief makes you feel helpless, lost, isolated, and like you're losing your mind. Early on, when someone would ask me what my day looked like, I would respond, "Breathe." This would come off as sarcasm, but it was anything but. I never imaged being a human could be so difficult. My body knew how to live, breathe, and stay alive; it had been doing it mostly on its own for thirty years. But suddenly existing felt like a new job I was unqualified for, and I wasn't going to be making employee of the month anytime soon.

In the weeks following Hank's death, I found myself finally sitting with the reality of what had happened, and nothing was left. I went from non-stop high stakes mayhem to nothingness. All that was left of my life was ruins. I tend to speak in absolutes and dramatics, but I genuinely felt like I just returned home from a war - battered, frail, traumatized, and fundamentally changed. I was able to experience being a mother for only a blink of an eye before it was ripped away. I had everything I could ever want right in front of me, and I couldn't have it. He was gone, and with him, all my purpose.

The emotional warfare began to manifest itself physically in the weeks following. I'm not sure which symptoms corresponded with grief, depression, anxiety, postpartum or surgery – or from a mixture of them all happening at once. my body felt like a Molotov cocktail.

As humans, we're somewhat aware of the psychological effects that typically go together with tragedy. However, the physical impacts are often discounted. This level of uncomfortableness was unexpected and unwelcomed.

"The body is equipped with innate tools meant to keep us safe. One of the most well-known (and essential) is the fight or flight response. This response system is designed to send signals to the body and brain when danger is perceived. Sometimes, the fight or flight response misfires, or is activated when there is no longer danger. This often occurs in people who have past trauma or have experienced long periods of intense stress. The heightened stress causes the body to be conditioned to experience fight or flight mode - where their stress response is essentially stuck in the "on" position. This means the nervous system can go into overdrive, all the adrenaline flooding the body has nowhere to go or no way to be expended." (Micah Abraham, "Coping with Anxiety and Restlessness", *CalmClinic.com,* 2020.)

This state of overdrive resulted in a few notable symptoms:

Painful Nerves: Times of high anxiety can cause nerve firing as well as increased blood flow to your extremities, resulting in heat, pain, and tingling to radiate through these pathways.

Increased Body Temperature: Anxiety often pairs with increased heart rate and vasoconstriction (narrowing of the blood vessels). This is typical for when the body is preparing for fight or flight, but when it remains stuck in that state for a prolonged period, it can drastically affect body temperature and regulation.

Hypertension: Aka, high blood pressure. Surges of anxiety can cause blood pressure to spike, putting your body in a state of stress.

Restlessness: One of the more common side effects of anxiety, restlessness is a direct result of that fight or flight activation. The excess adrenaline makes you feel a constant urge to keep moving, making it difficult to sit, remain still, or even attempt to relax.

Dilated Pupils: A small, but uncontrollable physical symptom resulting from the adrenaline rush.

Gastrointestinal Problems: This one's no secret. Times of stress, especially grief, lead many to food aversion or increase, and causes gastrointestinal problems. Emotional distress plays a major influence on our body's digestive system, and vice versa.

Sleep Disturbance: Another point from Captain Obvious here, but stress and anxiety cause major disruptions in sleep pattern. This is a tough one, since sleep is just about the only break your brain gets in grief, and it desperately needs it.

Why am I describing these symptoms to you? Why does it matter if my pupils were dilated? It's not like I cared, or that it's even interesting. I want to describe these to you because in my personal case, I did not in any way understand what was happening to me mentally *or* physically. Everything was haywire, and I was scared my body was just giving up. I was so incredibly uncomfortable not just from my emotional state, but by what was happening with me physically. I think acknowledging that these symptoms are medically common for an individual going through extreme turmoil brands them as somewhat less scary. By analyzing grief with a scientific lens, you can try to rationalize these unfamiliar and uncomfortable sensations and understand that your body is doing what it's supposed to in order to get back to baseline.

However, once the anxiety started to let up, depression stole the show. *Conveniently for us all*, depression and anxiety have a very high comorbidity - meaning they often will occur together, with one triggering the onset of another. If anxiety is described as chaos, depression would be its antithesis.

Most people who've never experienced depression would use it synonymously with sadness - it's not. Sadness would have been a relief. True depression is the absence of emotion and purpose. You view the world as a scary, meaningless place, and life as a chore you didn't sign up for. Life is muted, and depression does a very, very good job of making you think this version of your life is your forever.

I have unfortunately (or perhaps fortunately, in this circumstance), have had a run in with major depression before in my life. I was twenty-four at the time and had no idea what was happening to me. I had a good life with a bright future, so it didn't make sense to me why I was feeling the way I was. What I most recall about this experience is being terrified of having to live the rest of my life stuck feeling that way. I was in this mental state for about 8 months before I was able to gain back some sense of normalcy, which I attribute greatly to the help of medication. Before trying to start a family, where I expected an average pregnancy, delivery, and healthy baby, I was cautious about how my brain would handle postpartum. I was always on guard of falling back down the rabbit hole.

I felt the fog of depression starting to creep its way in days after I gave birth. The way I describe it best for me personally is like an on/off switch, there's not much in-between. I view the world in a completely different light and the way I process life changes. Exactly like a filter – but instead of making everything look brighter and better, it does the exact opposite. It was held at bay for a few weeks, but its presence was becoming eminent. It was like that switch started flickering a little at a time, until it became more frequent. I knew once it flipped, it was going to be very hard to reverse it, especially under these circumstances.

When it did flip it felt like it tripped the circuit breaker. It was crippling. I could not interact or function in the world. Honestly, if lobotomies were still around, I would have been first in line. My thoughts were dark and insistent. I felt mentally paralyzed, so much so that I was physically suffering. I remember exhausting every effort at one point to put one foot in front of the other to walk. My brain was broken.

It felt like I took the red pill from the *Matrix* and now saw the world as the melancholy place it really, truly was, and it was just everyone else who was in denial. To be direct, I didn't like it here, and I could no longer understand the point of it all. Death, divorce, sickness, hardships - suffering seemed to be everywhere, and I couldn't see the light.

However, having that experience of dealing with depression before, I had the wherewithal to know it *is* a temporary state of being. Wildly uncomfortable, but temporary. Now, that wasn't *all* that helpful, seeing that this time around, even if I did heal, my son would be forever gone. It was a reality I truly could not wrap my head around, and a place I wasn't keen on getting back to. But I had all the support and was doing the absolute best I could to get myself better. Because despite this scary perspective on the world, I deep down knew I still had a life well worth fighting for, so much so that I was persistently exhausting every effort to get well. This perfectly exemplifies how a brain can lie to you in a state of depression. I got on medication, put into therapy, joined a support group, expressed myself with healthy outlets, leaned heavily on loved ones, and held on for dear life.

I remember an initial doctor's appointment during this time, in efforts to get me help - I don't remember much of the discussion, but I do remember a woman telling me, "I see you coming out the other side of this." It sticks out to me because at that moment, I *honestly* did not believe her. She didn't know how much I was hurting, the emotional warfare I was going through. How was she so confident when she didn't know me?

But I'm writing to tell you that she was right about me, and I'm right about you. You will come out on the other side of this. It may seem impossible right now, but you will.

Navigating the Storm

"No one would have crossed the ocean if he could have gotten off the ship in the storm."
- Charles Kettering

Grief has a gravitational pull. It's self-centered and will draw everything around you into it. Not only do you have to make sense of living without this person, but life doesn't make it easy on you. It's decisions and practicalities, and watching the world continue to spin for those around you while yours is frozen. Grief takes a toll not only on your physical and mental wellbeing, but your finances, job, and relationships. There is a lot of collateral damage.

I remember being caught off guard when I was initially asked about funeral arrangements. I was so laser-focused on the tasks at hand in the hospital that I didn't even realize a funeral was also part of losing our son. At thirty, my husband and I had to decide an eternal resting place for him, and in turn for us. We thought we were going to be starting our life with its most exciting chapter, instead, we skipped ahead the whole book to the very end. I had to plan a wake, coordinate with the flower shop and funeral home, decide what type of service I wanted, what kind of speaker, whether it should be public or private to memorial collages from the few photos I had taken, and use what should have been his going home outfit and nursery sign, instead as pieces of his memorial display. The juxtaposition was unnerving.

I sat up the night before his funeral, making a poster board of the photos I had of him, and bills started to come in from the hospital. *They waste no time.* I remember opening the first envelope and sitting there in silence. I felt a weight settle on my chest, like an elephant just found itself a seat. My husband and I had planned well, and set ourselves up to be able to provide for a child. Now, on top of losing him, I was afraid our accounts would be drained by medical bills. Despite this not being the case for us, with insurance and loved ones stepping in, it's important to acknowledge that it *is* the case for many people who experience tragedy. Medical bills, legal costs, and memorial services are not only emotionally draining, but also financially draining.

It should all be the last sort of things you're concerned with, but tragedy doesn't work like that. In death, when it rains it pours. Once you survive the initial wave of daunting responsibilities, the real grief shows up. You will have to constantly confront reminders of your person, both tangible and theoretical. The life I thought I was about to have was taunting me everywhere I turned.

What were we supposed to do with his nursery? It seemed very trivial considering the circumstance, but we had everything in its place. Our home was left perfect to welcome him home. His clothes were hung, monitor charged, bedding washed, diapers lined up, every single thing was meticulously organized for a new, happy family of three. My husband hand built a crib, the aroma of wood stain still lingering. Things done out of love and expectation now felt like salt in a wound. I debated ripping it all down, but it was all I had left. Even now, with it feeling more so like a time capsule of a past life, I enter that space differently, and use it to reminisce - it feels like a representation of Hank despite him never entering it.

During the initial weeks, time when I was barely getting by, when I was living minute to minute, not one thing in the outside world mattered. Small grievances that bend you out of shape in typical life didn't exist, or not that they didn't exist, no energy was given to them. I wasn't participating in the small talk of society. My focus was to breathe, eat, and sleep. I went back to basics. I know it sounds strange, but despite being in anguish, I deep down wanted to remember this form of existence and the simplistic nature of it.

When I eventually began to face the world again, re-acclimating was challenging. Initially, I felt I was avoided like the plague. Panic would immediately set off in the eyes of anyone who saw me. I couldn't blame them; it was a difficult topic to breach. Whether it was a co-worker, acquaintance, or even a friend. No-one knew the proper way to interact with me. No-one wanted to mention it, for fear doing so would bring sadness. I tried to address the topic first, hoping to avoid some uncomfortableness. As time moved on, the awkwardness lifted with those close to me, but it would often make a surprise guest appearance with strangers.

"Do you have children?" I originally made a promise to myself that I would never lie about Hank when asked, but it was a promise I couldn't keep. In the times I would vocalize that yes, I did have a son, it wasn't worth the accompanying awkwardness. So, I would either end up feeling guilty for not mentioning him, or I would feel guilty for making the person in front of me uneasy when they'd be doing nothing more than engaging in innocent small talk. Lose-lose. Do what's best for you - and it may change with time, or conversation. I've quite literally have had this question asked of me twice in the same day and given different responses for each. Don't set strict expectations on yourself; it's more than okay to handle situations as they come.

I will say this though - and I feel as if others in these situations would agree; Even though the human response is to avoid the pain and try to continue with life as it was before, we *want* to talk about our lost loved ones. Any time anyone brought up Hank, I was filled with appreciation and joy, not sadness. Hearing his name spoken out loud by someone other than me was such caring reminder of his existence.

As that gravitational pull gets stronger, it's important to give grace, but it is undeniably hard not to become resentful when your pain seems to eclipse everyone else's. If you are a mother, it's a fact, your grief will be the worst after losing a child. Your sorrow, if measurable, engulfs everything. From the very moment I saw those two lines, my life was about him. Watching everything I put in my body, counting kicks, preparing his room and outfits, test driving strollers, constantly talking to him and making promises for when he reached the outside. To everyone else he was nine days old, but I knew him longer than that. We were in this together, until only one of us was left. These were my sacrifices made, and I didn't want to share my grief.

But we do have to share it, we must be conscious of that pull, and its effect on others. When we saw the writing on the wall of my son's prognosis, and knew we were going to lose him, I was terrified about what it meant for my marriage. My husband and I have different demons we both struggle with like every other human on this planet. I didn't know, and was honestly afraid to see how they would manifest in tragedy - especially of this magnitude. Fortunately, we came out much stronger, with a deeper appreciation for one another. We had officially seen each other in the darkest of times, and yet made the other a priority. We held one another accountable while also giving space and forgiveness. Relationship advice depends on the couple, but what I did learn - which was crucial - is to lean into love and to understand that people grieve differently. It's so important to allow each other to grieve differently. Some want to let it out, and some want to keep it in. Some become softer, and some become hardened. They call it a grieving process, because that's what it is, it's an ever-evolving undertaking. Try not to project expectations. When your own pain is all consuming, it's so hard to be understanding and forgiving of others, especially those closest to us, but it is so important to remember you are not the only person hurting. Your partner, family, and loved ones have also suffered an immense loss. Be cognizant of that. I don't say that to help your reputation, but because this understanding will help you heal yourself, and it will keep you moving forward in the right direction.

I'm self-aware enough to understand that it was not the easiest to be close to me during this time. Not necessarily because I was being difficult, but because life was being difficult. This chapter of life was supposed to be full of excitement not just for me - but everyone else as well. Being thirty and losing a child comes with its own set of complications beyond grief. I felt that I had lost a lot, and I didn't want my relationships to also suffer. I desperately wanted to maintain my normalcy and partake in the monumental moments being experienced by those around me, but it took much more effort than I think outsiders realized. I was reminded of my losses *everywhere* I turned. It's maybe an unpopular opinion but I don't think you should shy away from difficult or uncomfortable scenarios in life. I believe this for a few reasons. First, I didn't think it was fair to others. Second, I fundamentally knew that avoidance was not going to be a productive way to heal myself, and third and very importantly, I did not want to miss out on these big life moments. I really did and still do very much enjoy celebrating for others. But happiness and sadness are not mutually exclusive, *(more on this later)*. Even though I could swear in a court of law that my happiness for family and friends getting pregnant, having children, and watching them grow was wholeheartedly genuine, it also was just such a harsh reminder of the desolate situation I was personally in. It felt like I was putting in so much work, sacrifice, and carrying so much pain. I felt worn out from being reminded every single day of the raw deal I was handed. But I certainly didn't want this journey for any of my loved ones. I firmly believe having a child is the most magical moment in this hard life, and I refused to have that excitement dimmed for anyone due to my own misfortune. But it was hard. Despite what I did or said, I felt like I was sucking the air out of most rooms. And I was also the elephant in most of those rooms. My sheer presence evoked awkwardness. Am I making some of these feelings bigger in my mind than they were in reality? I'm sure, at times. But that doesn't change the fact that they were there. It became lonely.

I felt isolated after the loss of my son, but I never felt lonely until life continued to move on all around me as I was stuck. I'm not making a comparison, because life doesn't work like that, and you never should compare your life to anyone else's. But for the first time, I felt an intense sense of loneliness. I felt detached, and unrelatable. It was a touchy subject, and it makes sense. It's water that starts out as muddy. Getting pregnant and having children was *the* topic of conversation, it made up a large majority of what was going on in the world around me. I didn't want anyone to treat me differently, yet I also didn't want them to forget our suffering. It's like needing to be invited to something but not wanting to go - *which we all can relate to.* I didn't want attention, but I wanted to be seen, I at least wanted the pain of the situation to be seen. I didn't want Hank's life to go unnoticed, especially when other babies were being born and getting celebrated daily.

In reality though, I didn't want the children who belonged to other people. I didn't want other people's lives. I wanted mine, or what mine should have been. It made it much easier to watch on the sidelines when I understood that what they were getting wasn't actually what I wanted. I'd had what I wanted; it was just for a brief time. That's such a hard concept to come to terms with, but eventually, you will be grateful for that time, no matter how short, or unfair, and it will be yours and no one else's.

This goes for everyone experiencing the loss of a loved one. It will always sting watching those connections continue on in the world when yours is broken, and forever gone. But no one in the world had that person. They were yours. That connection, that bond you shared with them, is sacred to you and just for you - and that love can't ever be taken away.

Hard Truths

"A lesson learned the hard way is a lesson learned for a lifetime."
- Anonymous

Questions that come to mind for almost every grieving person: why couldn't the tragedies of life leave us alone and allow us to be happy? Why couldn't it have been someone else? But it *was* me. It *is* us. It's a hard truth that's difficult to accept. In life, we only have actual control over so much.

If I were to pinpoint when I began to feel less fragile, it would be when I began to accept my situation. To be able to accept your reality for what it is without trying to reconstruct the past is critical to our healing and our ability to move forward in life with a sense of peace. Acceptance is a very important hard truth, and it certainly wasn't the only one I came face-to-face with in the aftermath of loss.

You are not alone. This phrase is typically one of comfort; and yes, I needed someone or something to relate to. But, at the same time it hurts to realize that this degree of heartache happens, and often. It's sad to realize that other people have been in this position before and know that others will be in the future. Hearing you're not alone can come across as diluting your pain. It's frustrating to compare your situation to anyone else's because it's personal, and it feels like no one has ever felt as bad as you do right now. But, in order to move forward it's important to understand that grief is universal, and you are not alone in this. That means you don't have to fight this alone, either. Yes, it will feel that way, but there are people out there willing and wanting to help, please ask for it.

People will say the wrong things. People will also do the wrong things. It's inevitable. Keep in mind that most people really are doing their best, and intention is everything. It was very hard for me to not become bitter in those moments, especially when someone would deliver my personal favorite eye roll-inducing credo that *"everything happens for a reason"*. You expect everyone to understand the situation, but they don't, and they never will. Even I, while writing a book about loss, cannot fully relate to your specific circumstances. You can see something bad happen from the outside, but until you're in the front row, you can't really have a profound understanding of it. Remind yourself that people are providing support the best way they know how and view it in a positive light. Accept their words with grace, because even
though people will say the wrong things, they will also say the *right* things. You will be surprised by how compassionate humans are if you let them be. Do not underestimate your need for support. I was absolutely awestruck at the support and genuine kindness that we received. Support saved me - not just literally, but the sincerity of family, friends, and strangers saved me from feeling resentful. I felt seen. My pain felt seen. Very few people met Hank, and yet they expressed his importance as a person. I will never forget it. On the harder days, I reminisce

on that love and compassion, and remind myself of all the good there is out there.

You'll become a final girl. For those who aren't familiar with the horror genre, "final girl" refers to the last girl alive to confront the killer, the one left to tell the story. The one that people speculate about and wonder what it must have been like for her to live through the terror. People love bad news, often more than good news; it's just human nature. I theorize it's because it's such a reminder of how lucky you are to not be that person, an affirmation that you have so much to be thankful for. When human beings hear about other people's tragedies, we look on, rubbernecking, forming theories of the situation in gossip circles. I felt like I became a cautionary tale. Friends of friends or family I'm sure were bringing it up in their circles of gossip, "I know a girl who…". No matter the reasons behind it, bad news does in fact spread like wildfire. It's not until you're the person suffering through the bad news that you become acutely aware of the strangeness of it all. Here you are. You are a final girl. You confronted the monster of grief and made it out alive. You fought and survived. You made it out to tell your story; and in that story your loved one lives on.

Holidays will be difficult. That goes for all events. I lost Hank a week before Thanksgiving. That day family and friends stopped over intermittently, dropping off gifts, hugs, and platters of turkey dinner that I couldn't stomach. Despite all the love, I felt as if I would die from a broken heart that day. Come Christmas time, instead of the picture-perfect new family image that should have been sent out on our holiday cards, my husband and I bore more of a resemblance to Billy Bob Thornton in Bad Santa. We did what we could to get through that season - and you should, too. Be gentle with yourself and go easy on the expectations. Life isn't going to look like you imagined it would, and major life events are where the starkest contrast takes place.

On that same note, however, some days when I was braced for impact were nothing like I thought they would be. Mother's Day, both our birthdays…I would feel on edge in the weeks and days leading up to them, but when they would arrive, they were far more manageable than expected. Just because you feel a certain day in itself should be sad, it doesn't mean it has to be. I never felt obligated to lock myself in a room and cry just because it was the anniversary of a certain day. I think this was surprising not only to me, but also to others. People tend to think you grieve with a cartoon rain cloud over your head, but if you feel fine, stable, or even happy, go with it. I found the unpleasant feelings will more often rear themselves on a random, uneventful day. Allow yourself to feel what you feel at face value, and don't feel a need to analyze why.

You can't rewrite the past. After I gave birth, I was stuck at my delivering hospital for a few days, then decided to sleep the next few nights at home. Having just had a cesarean, I should have been sleeping on something more supportive than a couch in the NICU, but that was half an excuse I gave myself. I look back at this time with regret over not constantly being by my son's side. To amplify my guilt, on the mornings I woke up at home, I didn't want to go back to Children's hospital. I loved Hank so much, but I couldn't handle physically or emotionally what the day would bring. We were in the midst of tests, and theorizing what was wrong, and no prognosis brought hope. I purposely wanted to miss the doctors' rounds because I was terrified of what they were going to say. I knew something was critically wrong, and I didn't want to hear it spoken out loud. I wasn't ready for the small optimism left to be shattered. The human brain doesn't like an unknown, particularly when all the unknowns are bad. I wanted to get in a car and leave my life behind. It's as simple and as complicated as that. Thankfully, my husband never left Hank's side; he was unwavering. He was there when I couldn't be. I find extreme comfort in knowing that Hank was taken care of, never left alone, and loved so deeply in those first nights when I wasn't there. I will forever be grateful to my husband for giving me that peace.

I certainly don't share this secret because I'm proud of it - nor do I share it to be self-deprecating. I share it because I am unquestionably not the only one in my situation who has felt this way, and I want to say it's okay. The human body and soul can only handle so much at once, my fight or flight was kicking in, and I had no fight left. It wasn't until around day five that I was able to regain some semblance of control and be the mom I thought I would be. I am forgiving of myself during this time because I know I genuinely was doing the best I could. You will always have regrets about things you did or didn't do during loss. This is truly unprecedented territory for anyone. Be kind to yourself and know that you did your best, and your best is more than enough.

Happiness and sadness are not mutually exclusive. There's no right time to be happy again. You may feel shame when you laugh again for the first time. Don't. There's no right time - or to put it another way, there's no wrong time to laugh and smile again. It didn't seem fair that I was able to experience joy again when I knew Hank had never been able to. If he couldn't be here, I felt guilty being anything but miserable. Please though, don't give up on life, and don't give up on celebrating. Will it feel pointless and sometimes painful? Yes, but lean into things you used to enjoy. There is a healing that comes from not letting your loss control your life or take away more joy than it already has. You don't have to be outwardly sad in order to show people that you're grieving - they know. This hard truth also made me feel like a walking contradiction. I'm so grateful for what I have left, but I also feel resentful over how much has been taken away. It's a constant push-pull, an emotional rollercoaster I'm still riding on. My hope is that one day, the dips and loops will get less severe, and I can move to the kiddie section.

Life is not fair. This may be the hardest one. Life will chew you up and spit you out, but I don't have to tell you that. We all, deep down, despite knowing how life works, have the wholesome idea that things will work out for us. That we will get the fairytale ending. Having that theory disproved is *so* disheartening. Fundamentally, life is not fair, it will be a massive disappointment at times, and there is no way around that. Bad things happen to good people, and often - and good things happen to those who don't deserve them. Now, before you close this book because I've officially killed the mood, let me explain why this hard truth is actually of value. It grants you the freedom of the now. Learn to live in the present and be grateful for the things that are going right, no matter how small. Grab onto what you have left with a fierce passion. I appreciate small moments I would have previously overlooked. Mundane normalcy is a gift not many people realize until it's gone. Life doesn't keep score, and you never know what tomorrow will bring, so savor the now. You never know -

even in the depths of despair, something incredible, and beautiful can be right around the corner.

Time is Tricky: As more time passes, I could tell you it gets easier, and I technically wouldn't be lying - because it does, but it gets challenging in other ways. The memories are no longer fresh, seasons change, the cards and flowers stop coming in. The shock will begin to fade, though, and the days will feel more bearable. Life goes on - as it should. We're not supposed to be stuck in a chapter of life, no matter how much we may want to hold onto it. Moving forward is painful, but necessary. Doing that doesn't mean you are leaving your person behind. And it's true, despite it being a slow process, time does heal.

You are responsible for your healing. *Yikes*, I know. You will be allowed to wallow in self-pity for however long and no one will stop you because it's warranted. No one will be the first to say it's time to keep moving forward - so it must be you. How do you begin to do so when it was exhausting work to just hang on? It was very scary to know I was the one who had to break myself out of this mental prison. You must make the decision to do the work and adjust your mindset to change what you've lost into what you've had. How you perceive the world and react to it is up to you, despite having valid reasons to be bitter. It is also incredibly frustrating to heal from something that isn't your fault. But you *can* do this.

But how? I follow up each hard circumstance I've described here by saying that I eventually began to heal, but how? How do you get to acceptance? How do you play an active role in your healing, especially when you don't necessarily want to? Well, I wrote this book to help others - and what advice can I give? What tools can I provide? I'm not a qualified professional in any of these aspects. I've told my story, but I'm one individual - and although loss is universal, as I mentioned many times before this, humans navigate it differently.

I fortunately found a psychotherapist while I was in the depths of grief who understood my brain and personality. She helped me dissect the complexity of my mental distress. I was able to learn that my feelings, however unpleasant, were normal. As we continued sessions throughout my healing journey, I wished others could be privy to her words.

Well, listen up.

Your Brain and Grief

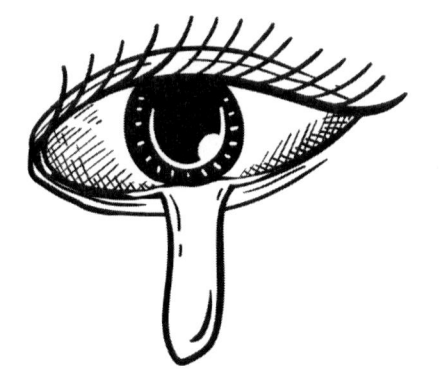

Megan Hedglen, LPC, NCC, M.Ed.
Co-Founder of "The Therapy Collective"

As far as grief goes, I've got to say, it's one of my least favorites to work on in therapy. Now, that comes strictly from my feelings about helping my clients in a direct way. I'd say most of the time, people come to therapy and sit, looking at me across a table and they want real skills. Issues like OCD, anxiety, and depression make providing help easier. For example, there is a clear understanding that if you have a phobia of heights, we have to challenge it. Or, if you have panic attacks, we can learn techniques of how to ground and distract ourselves during an episode. Grief is a different beast.

Grief allows us as therapists a chance to teach coping skills, but that's just a watered-down term for acceptance. Accepting the loss of someone who very much belongs in your life creates anger in a client at the beginning of their grief journey. As it should. Hurting people want the pain to stop; and they want real, concrete steps to follow to navigate toward feeling whole again. Well, it's hard. It's really hard to look someone in the eyes at a very pivotal time of life and tell them there is no plan. Even further, that a real plan would make things harder and isn't plausible. To go even further, that they themselves aren't ready to feel whole again yet. And just in case that isn't difficult enough, to then also say there's a portion of them that wants to be in that pain. See, I bet it's not difficult to understand why I struggle to like the beginning portions of grief work with my clients. Stick with me, though. The end is bright(er), and people do feel better - eventually. Eventually, everyone feels better. Even if you do everything "wrong," not that there is such a possibility; you will feel better.

The good news is that there are some things you can do to speed up the process of feeling whole again. Therapy can help you understand and navigate reasons for the feelings you are experiencing, making growth a side effect of the anguish. Being that I'm sure I have frustrated at least some of you by now, but let me see if I can now be concise and helpful, and make it up to you.

Grief is a medicine. I think the beginning portion of almost all treatment is understanding. I mean, it's like going into a boxing match; you want to know who and what you're up against, right? So, knowledge, an understanding of how and why grief can take over can give us a fighting chance. People hate when I tell them grief is medicine, and I don't blame them. It's a confusing statement that feels like it should be written beneath the welcome image on a Facebook support group page. But to analyze it is impactful to understanding what grief does to us and our mind.

When we are grieving, we are very much spending time with the person we lost. Yes, I will admit, it's not really "quality time". But it's the best we can get, isn't it? Missing someone is the second-best thing to having them around. When we can't have someone anymore, we spend time with the shadow of that person - that is grieving. Shadows are dark and cold, and they remind us of how not-dark and not-cold the world was before the person we're missing was gone. Even so, that is all we have of our person and so we stay. We think about them in the earliest hours of the morning when we wake up aching and alone. We think about them when we laugh really hard, too. But in thinking of them; it brings more pain. It's easy to see how the cycle of grief can be hard to overcome. We think not to hurt and then that reminds us we are hurting. Regardless of the futility here, it's important to understand why and what grieving is to us before we can move on. And so, if you're reading this, try to adopt some awareness of the reasoning behind your pain and thoughts. Try to remember that you are spending as much time with that person as you can - even if it hurts you, even if it isn't good enough. Grief is a medicine because it is the only way to be with our loss. It hurts to think about the way that person smells, the way they touched our lives, or even what they missed out on. Grief is a medicine because we long to think of it, even if it hurts.

When our life provides us with an absence, we try to fill it. The best analogy feels too simple. It pales in comparison to how you are feeling, but it does help convey an understanding of it. So, bear with me through this; eye rolling is allowed. Think of misplacing something that you really liked - maybe a pair of sunglasses. At first, you spend a *lot* of time looking for these sunglasses; after all, you *just* had them. You're on the way out the door and can't imagine not having them the whole day. You're looking in drawers, the refrigerator, and you just can't seem to leave until you find them. Now you're twenty minutes late, and there are places to be, so eventually you get in the car and go about your day. But that doesn't mean they're off your radar. The rest of the week, you're listening to people talk, going to work, sitting at a coffee shop, and your mind floats to where they could be. When you're busy, it's not so bad - but when the light shines just right, and you're driving down the road, you still check your car for them - just in case. Eventually, time does go by and you think about where they could have gone less and less often. Every once in a while, though, something jogs your memory. You see a picture of yourself from the summer two years back and they're right there on your face. At this point you have accepted them not being a part of your day-to-day life anymore and you admire the picture from a different angle. We can learn to accept something's absence, eventually; but at first, your brain looks for it a *lot*.

Grieving and "looking for" something or someone is much deeper than that, of course. That being said, it *is* similar in a far larger context. The constant pain you are feeling right now, that is you recognizing a loss and there is a very heavy constant reality that you cannot find a way to fix the loss. Nonetheless, you spend time missing the person you've lost because it's the only way to have them around until you can live without them. The kind of grief that comes later down the road, once there is more acceptance, brings with it an appreciation of when we had our person, before the loss. Grief is a medicine because it leads us to acceptance.

You will hear a lot about the stages of grieving when you are going through loss. Because of that, I don't want to use the little time I have here to talk at length about them. I trust your Google skills. I reference the stages of grieving to talk at length about one - acceptance. When someone talks about feeling better after time and a loss, they're referring to acceptance. I don't think that's the same "better" that someone is looking to feel when they first come into my office, though. I believe the initial need for help involves getting their head above water - because initially, it feels impossible to survive the loss. So, let's look at that next.

Loss, Trauma, and PTSD: Losing someone can feel traumatic, losing someone can be traumatic, and losing someone can cause PTSD. Please note that these are all *very* different things. The larger part of those who grieve are grieving something that feels traumatic but it is not actually considered a trauma to their brain. Then, there are those who are experiencing trauma but are exploring it in the appropriate and positive ways of coping. This means getting us to where we need to be without developing disordered thoughts surrounding the trauma. Many people can experience actual trauma and not develop PTSD. The majority, once again, cope without developing PTSD. The reason I am bringing this to the table is that the majority of people believe that experiencing trauma *always* leads to PTSD, and that experiencing a loss is *always* traumatic. This matters when you're not sure if you're on the right track with grieving. Is this trauma? Is this just loss and sadness - the grieving process in general? *Or*, is this something more, like disordered grieving or even PTSD? The specifics are difficult to negotiate, which is why seeing a professional is best. I'm hesitant to try to define the differences in any length here because I feel if you're even questioning it, you have good reason to see a professional. My experience with more complicated grief is that it is immensely receptive to therapy. Immensely.

They are interdependent on one another, as well. There is enough proof to assume that therapy can prevent complicated grieving and reduce the impact of trauma in relation to grieving. So, be proactive if you fear you are heading in a scary direction. In the long run, it can be seen as preventative. If you read the rest of this and feel like you're absolutely worse off, if you're grieving intensely enough to prevent taking care of yourself, or if you have thoughts of harm or suicide, please make an appointment immediately. Just as importantly, if you did make or do make an appointment and then do not feel comfortable with or helped by that person, make a new one. I tell my clients that they might not need to feel a connection with their optometrist, but they should feel one with their therapist. We are used to people moving on, and you should call someone new if you didn't get the help you needed. Keep on looking. Think of it like picking out a book for yourself; that's how you should view picking a therapist. If the content isn't for you, move on. If the concepts aren't for you, move on. If you feel judgment or above the material they have to offer, move on. Someone will help you and speak to your soul differently.

What does healthy loss look like in the beginning?

Our Responses to Grief: A Mental and Psychological Look: It's no surprise that grief takes a toll on us in an emotional way; it impacts our mental health a lot. When someone talks about the way they are feeling when they are grieving, we don't often think about the physical impact; we picture someone crying on their couch for hours, not holding their head in pain. But you can see where I am going here: we experience both. As I mentioned above, one of the largest benefits of therapy for the griever involves understanding what is happening to them and within them. My emphasis on education continues in this section for that very reason.

An article published in *The Psychiatric Times* reported that 40 percent of grievers qualify to meet the criteria of major depression during the first month after their loss. Nearly 25 percent still qualify after two months. So, this means that immediately following a loss, someone is highly likely to be experiencing the symptoms of depression. I would be willing to bet these numbers are an underestimate, as most people don't make their way into treatment. Although it is true that a portion do become clinically depressed, they cannot be diagnosed until after those two months. This is because to feel this way is so *expected*, so typical, that a griever feeling depression is viewed as an adaptive part of the grieving process - a necessary mountain to climb before they can expect to feel better. This means we need to ride out the pain, gradually work toward acceptance, and deal with the symptoms of depression (and sometimes anxiety) as a means of healthy grieving. Simply put, even if you're doing it right and as healthy as possible, it will feel like you're sick and that you're doing it wrong. That is, again, why education matters so much. Knowing that you're on the right path matters when you're in pain.

As we continue to explore the mental distress associated with grief, we'll talk about some things that are "normal" as we work toward acceptance. After all, that's the basis of support groups in full. There is a term we use for this in therapy: catharsis. Basically, there is healing and profound relief in hearing that others feel similar to how we do. We are not alone. We are not weird. We are certainly not the only ones thinking this way. Being alone in our thoughts adds to the distress of feeling depression during grief. The list below is not comprehensive, but it definitely touches on what I see most frequently in my office.

I'm acting like nothing happened. It's easy to do, and denial is one of the steps of grief. Not everyone hits every step, but it is totally normal to struggle to accept that anything happened at all. A lot of times, people take this idea very literally, thinking that someone is actually acting as if the loss never happened. That does happen from time to time, but it's not common. What I see more often is people waking up in the mornings and forgetting for an instant and then realizing all over again that someone is gone. Another, similar scenario is that they think that person is alive for just a second. They'll think to text that person when something funny happens, or they feel tomorrow will have the person in it until they remember that person is not here. This kind of forgetting and remembering is jolting to most people; they feel like they're "losing it." But it is mostly normal and goes away fairly quickly. It's a brain accident. We let our guard down, and here we are coming to terms all over again with the idea that someone isn't with us anymore.

Another aspect of this reaction involves entrenching ourselves in distractions. From the outside looking in, it can seem like the grieving person is moving on too quickly. Back to work, back to school, back to planning a vacation, back to paying bills, back to keeping a house, back to wanting to try again for another child...You get my drift, right? Here, we see the person who is grieving either never fully starts or is taking a break using distractions and new challenges. This can also be very typical in the grieving process. People need to take a break from pain. Sometimes they don't start right away because they aren't ready. Grief is a different journey for everyone, and some people's early actions can come across as confusing and cold to others. It's okay to feel this way, too; we usually make our way back needed to journey toward acceptance.

I'm blaming myself. Back when I was first learning about counseling and grief, I was told that with grief there is a natural feeling of guilt. This guilt can be divided into two categories: guilt for things I didn't do and wish I did, and guilt for things that I did do that I wish I didn't. Most people tell me the pain they are feeling involves some level of feeling guilty or that they had the power to have changed something. This does not always mean preventing the loss. It can also mean wishing they had done "better" in the person's life or "not taken them for granted." Sometimes people preoccupy themselves with self-blame or guilt because it's something to do. In a world that is very much outside of our control, it sometimes makes more sense to find a reason for hurt. Blaming oneself gives the brain some level of preoccupation, and the need to do this is a normal part of grieving for a good portion of people. It is also allowing the brain to accept the past as something that can no longer be changed. As we are working toward accepting the past and the future to get closer to fully processing our grief, it is important to remember the person who was lost. What would this person want for us? Asking these questions can create a conversation with our loss and remind us that guilt isn't helping.

Most of the time, people process this guilt rather quickly, as well. A natural awareness that there are things outside of our control does tend to arise.

I'm angry. It's normal to look around and want to find a reason. We look to find the source of our pain and what is causing it. If that isn't within us, it must be in the outside world. Sometimes, this shows up in a more general context, and sometimes it's anger specific to the loss. When someone is directly to blame for the loss that we are experiencing, whether it be due to medical malpractice, accident, or other avoidable wrongdoing, we review this at length. It's not fair, and it's often not expected. We, as people, struggle to make peace with it, because nothing can bring the person back. In therapy, the goal here is to allow the anger to not hide from it, and to do something that makes the anger useful. Processing our anger takes time. It feels better when we can try to "right the wrong". This can come in many forms. People who are angry in these contexts don't know where to direct their emotion, and we review that in therapy. Sometimes the answer is in starting a foundation, sometimes it's in writing a strongly worded letter, sometimes it's in filing a lawsuit, and sometimes it's in getting a punching bag to keep in the basement. It's completely okay to feel anger in grief, it's often a part of the stages of grief that I keep mentioning. Finding a place to put our anger that's healthy is the goal.

I'm so mad at my higher power. Here we are again, feeling anger. Anger at our higher power. Whether that higher power we answer to is God or karma, we think long and hard about our choices in life, in the ultimate hope that they pay off. Do good things, and good things happen to you - this is something most of us are raised to believe. So, when bad things start happening, we feel absolutely abandoned and ignored. It's normal for our faith to be shaken. It's normal to take a break from believing. It's normal if we're not sure we want to keep trying to be good people. It's something you should take space with. Set boundaries with those in your life whom we might feel judged by at this time. This is okay to do. Ultimately, you have time to figure it all out.

Adding additional guilt and confusion creates a bigger problem.

I don't feel anything. A sense of numbness is also common at some point in the "grief journey." Depression sometimes exhibits itself in symptoms of numbness; and, as I previously mentioned, grief and depression go hand in hand. In a more contextual way, when we are grieving, we sometimes don't feel the same as we used to. Life's colors can be muted, feelings can be dulled, and sounds don't have the same ring that they once did. This can be alarming when it happens, especially if two days before, we were feeling too much. It's scary to go from feeling like a powder keg of tears and rage to not caring about anything anymore. I think what I notice is the most confusing thing for someone who is grieving is the radical changes from one day to the next. A person may feel more capable in their grief from one day to the next. The journey isn't up or downhill. Grief skips around and progresses with grief, and acceptance does the same.

I can't feel anything else. Like not feeling anything, feeling completely tied to the grieving is also alarming and something to prepare for. While it sounds typical for the beginning moments of grief, and it often is, it's also possible to feel entrenched in grief a month or more later. These days are long and seem unrelenting. This is where we may note an impact on things like hygiene, weight, maintaining other relationships, holding down a job, and sustaining other responsibilities. It is vitally important to know if we are in this place. If we're here - it is time to seek help. Professional help can determine a short-term or longer-term course of medication when necessary. In addition, we should allow other things back into our life at a manageable pace. Usually, when people get back to doing a bito9i more, they begin to feel better. Rest and a lack of interaction sounds like good medicine; unfortunately, they aren't. Feeling other things is hard after a loss, but it does help us to move forward and build acceptance to living in our new world.

I don't like being around people. Again, with the anger and guilt?! Yes, yet again. Grief can make us want to shelter in place from friends, family, and coworkers. The people this reaction impacts most when they are otherwise social creatures; it's like they recognize the change and feel guilt for not being available. Taking time away from people is okay, whether you're typically a loner or not. Sometimes, we know intrinsically what we need to get better. Other times, we need a push in the opposite direction. It's important to check in with others. That being said, people can be a huge trigger for someone in active grief. I've thought a lot about how to explain the typical frustrations with others during a time of grieving - but I think paraphrasing the most common ones may be more helpful:

"People don't know what to say; they treat me differently."

"I don't know what to say. I feel bad that they feel bad for me."

"People are worried about such trivial things, and it annoys me."

"People are acting like nothing even happened."

"People are pushing me to spirituality or grief groups."

"People are nosy - and I haven't even spoken to them in years."

"People don't know how good they have it."
"I feel anger and jealousy."

"People don't know what I am going through."

While the above list is in no way exhaustive, it's a good representation of what's typical. People immediately feel guilt reporting the above, and we work a ton on boundaries in almost every session. It's totally normal to want to take space. My advice? Be as honest as you can in setting boundaries and expectations; when it comes down to it, most people just want to be helpful. It's my experience that most people miss the mark here when it comes to help and support because they don't know how to say nothing at all.

I don't like being alone. Let's face it. Being alone is scary - like, little kid, middle of the night scary. We all feel worse in the evening winding down for bed, whether that be from a normal cold or a very heavy feeling of sadness in your heart. We can attribute it to a lot of causes - but mainly, it's being tired and being alone. There is a *lot* of room to think when we're alone, when things are quiet; and thinking when you're grieving goes along with being aware of our loss. At night, there is a lot of time to review the could've, should've, would'ves. There's a lot of time to contemplate old memories and futures we will never get. The simple explanation here is that this is a normal brain avoiding normal brain work when it comes to grief. But that doesn't help much, does it? Just plain ole' "You're supposed to feel that way." isn't a very helpful method of coping. Instead, we should allow ourselves to distract. If we can't sleep, we get up and do something that feels better. Let it be TV, or a kickboxing workout at three in the morning. People intermingle distraction with repression and feel that almost all thoughts that come in should be fully processed. If you are working to refrain from being alone, you aren't ready to process, and that is okay. Distract yourself instead, because I said so and because you need a break.

Getting better involves being okay with being alone and allowing yourself space from the grief. This is a great time to challenge yourself to take time away from the person you've lost, as counterintuitive as that sounds. If you aren't ready, that's okay too. Call whomever is on the docket; the people in your life want to help. If that means having adult sleepovers for a while, that sounds cool to me. If that means calling someone at 2 a.m. to talk about the most recent comedy show you saw on Netflix, that also sounds cool to me. Being alone is not bad, and not wanting to be alone is not bad. Keep a lookout for isolation though. Get dressed and leave the house once a day. That *is* important. Keep in mind that you have to feel alive to get better, and you have to find small reasons to get better.

I'm mad at them for leaving me alone. Hell, I'm mad *for* you. It stings us with guilt when we are angry at someone who isn't here to stand up for themselves. It stings us with guilt when we look at the future, all the great smells and tastes and sounds and them not being here for that. Some people turn to anger when sadness feels overwhelming; and it is sometimes an easier emotion to feel. Anger usually comes at some point in the journey to acceptance. If you're mad right now, day to day, you're taking space from sadness. While this can become unproductive, it is a healthy way of processing to gain acceptance. Write a letter to your person if you're tired of feeling mad; I can almost promise that you'll be back to sadness in no time. Then, do what feels right with the letter. Roll your eyes if you want to, but letters help us process. It's one coping skill I actually get behind for grief, and I try to make each of my clients write more than one letter along the grieving process. You can see your development in your emotions in each letter. And if you want somewhere else to direct your anger, you can be mad at me. I don't mind helping out. I compared your grief and loss to losing sunglasses up there in my first section. I earned it.

I don't want to forget them. This is the big one. Let's go back to the ideals behind "grief is a medicine." Not only are we spending time with that person, but we are coming to know we are getting closer to acceptance, and we fear leaving grief; we don't feel "okay" leaving the remembrance of them. This makes some pretty complete sense. It's another step down in loss. Initially, when we lose someone, we feel ripped apart from this person, or the idea of what this person would be or could be, depending on the situation. Not now, though. Now, we are feeling more prepared to take our space. We have learned to be without them in the way we once were. What I notice now, more than ever, is a fear of loss or leaving in a more finite way. I think people are scared of acceptance. I think acceptance feels like we are saying, "I'm doing alright, I don't need that person anymore." Here are the common things I find myself saying to people when they're fearing the ideals behind acceptance:

- It does not mean you're happy to live without them.

- It does not mean you don't want to spend time grieving them.

- It does not mean you won't think about them anymore when that song comes on.

- It does not mean you are leaving their memory behind.

- It does not mean they will be disappointed to not be missed.

- It does not mean you are relieved when you begin to feel better.
  Let's dive into this one here for a bit.

I think people struggle ultimately with being comfortable in feeling better. More specifically, they wonder: what does it mean that I am feeling better? For some, this can happen almost right away, for some, this happens later down the road in the grief journey. It can be sudden or it can be slow; but it is always jarring to be happy to feel better. This is a natural and healthy part of the experience and something we can create some balance and control with. Now is the time to start investing in bringing in the memory of the person we've been grieving in a nostalgic, loving way. Let it flow, enjoy your day, eat a sandwich, laugh at a joke, mock your boss with work friends. There is plenty of time to get home and bring the "missing you" back into focus if you still need it. Light a candle for them, think about the plans you had for the future together, talk to them in the car (my personal favorite). At the end of the day, the goal is to feel better. At the end of the day, that will allow for happy tears. At the end of the day, that is what your person would want for you. I promise.

Processing Matters: Whether or not you're experiencing grief or something bigger, processing the events and the loss really matters. Processing the change, allowing it to seep into our consciousness - that is the goal. Processing is what assists and reduces PTSD, trauma, and loss in general. The more we talk, the more we explore it, the more we head toward accepting it. Again, grief is a medicine; our natural attempt is to process it. Processing is viewing it until it no longer sets off our "grief alarm" in our mind. It is allowing us to focus on it enough to feel we have edged toward acceptance, slowly. When we see people starting foundations in honor of their loved one, they are working on processing. When we see people talking incessantly about their loss, they are processing. When we see people sitting in the room of their lost loved one, they are processing. We naturally gravitate to processing, and we have a lot of "allowable options" that are healthy. They lead us toward acceptance. You're getting there, you're capable of making it there, you're working on it, I promise. What works for you in processing is different from what works for another. Like I said, I enjoy talking to my dad in the car. Some of us need to do something bigger, leaving an impact beyond just us and our person.

Some of us even write books.

No Rain No Flowers

"Tis better to have loved and lost than never to have loved at all."
- Lord, Alfred Tennyson

Flowers are given in times of loss and heartache, but also in celebrations and love. I love the duality that they provide, and how they are a constant reminder that love and sorrow have such a thin line between them.

Some people don't particularly like flowers; they think it is a waste to spend money on something that can't be enjoyed for very long. I never saw it that way. Flowers are a lot like life; they are beautiful and young only for a short time, and then - like all living things - they die. They provide a constant reminder that we need to acknowledge the beauty in life while it's here and hold onto those beautiful moments while we can. Our time here is limited, and we only get to bloom for so long.

What allows flowers to bloom? Rain, effort, time, but also sunlight and care – as in life. I would not be the same without experiencing all parts of it.

Often, during my storm, all I wanted was to be back to my normal life, before any of the loss happened. My new reality was too much to handle. Part of that suffocating feeling was that I knew nothing would ever be the same. I saw how quickly life could turn. I saw a darkness in life that I wish I never had. I knew that I would have to live the rest of my life grieving. I tried so hard to be the person I used to know, but I wasn't. In time though, I leaned into that change.

Allow yourself to change, I think you'll be proud of who you become. Tragedy recalibrates you. Despite the damage this loss has caused, I would never trade the pain for not knowing him. It doesn't make sense now, but once this cloud of anguish and bitterness begins to lift, you will emerge with a deeper understanding of the significance of this situation in your life journey.

It is very hard when something big and bad happens to not have it be made into your identity. It would be the first thing others would associate with me I'm sure, but it was also how I saw myself. Overnight my world got ripped apart and in that, my sense of self. And I'm not particularly helping my case, since he's passed I've made conscious efforts to make sure he's not forgotten. I held a 5k race and picnic the following summer. I was looking for an outlet and a way to keep him close, and it worked. It was a huge success - *shout out to all the Hank's Race participants and supporters*. I decided not to continue the race for a few reasons, mainly being I think it accomplished what I sought out to do with it. That day was for him, it was more his memorial than his funeral ever could or should have been. Also, I didn't want it to be an annual event that dwindled over the years until I eventually threw in the towel. However, I didn't want to stop advocating on his behalf. He still wasn't here, I was still grieving, and life was still throwing curveballs. I wanted to accomplish something with a more enduring impact.

I have learned a lot along this journey, I figured all this pain would maybe be worth something if I could share what I've learned with others. Do not confuse that with a silver lining. There is none in loss, especially baby loss. My son didn't die so I can stop and smell the roses. He died, and I want to help comfort anyone else who has had to endure similar pain. He died, and I desperately want to live a life he would be proud of.

Moving Forward for Them

If you've made it this far, figuratively, and literally, I hope you've found what you're looking for. I hope you've found solace. I hope you've found some light in the dark. Of all the advice, lessons, and metaphors this book holds, what I'm going to say next is what I most want you to remember.

If you can't move forward for you, do it for them. You are now your person's legacy. What you bring to the world is a reflection on them. Your time here, time that they no longer have, is *so* important. In the dark days, when you want to give up, remember them and keep moving forward. You'll be so glad you did.

Epilogue

"The laws of genetics apply even if you refuse to learn them."
- Allison Plowden

So, how did we get here? I wrote this book as a tool for others enduring a loss, and I didn't initially feel the need to go into the nitty gritty details of the miscarriages, or Hank's diagnosis. But as my story continued to unfold, my experiences became bigger than me, and the revelations important to share.

I'll say this first - It's common for people to decide not to get genetic testing before or during pregnancy because it wouldn't matter and that they would love the baby anyway. This is a very naive take on why genetic testing is important. We all love our babies. Genetic testing is a way to either prepare for medical complications a child may have, or to take away the possibility of that child suffering. Unfortunately, in this world, there are genetic disorders that not only take away quality of life, but also take away life itself. It's a reality. It doesn't mean that because a child isn't perfect your love for them waivers.

Hank's diagnosis of SMA type 0/1 fell into this category of life limiting. So, what is SMA? Spinal muscular atrophy is a genetic, progressive, neurodegenerative disease that affects the motor nerve cells in the spinal cord. These nerve cells cannot signal to the muscles, causing them to atrophy.

SMA is caused by a mutation in the survival motor neuron gene 1 (SMN1). In a healthy person, this gene produces a protein that is critical to the function of the nerves that control our muscles. Individuals with SMA produce low levels of survival motor neuron (SMN) protein. Without this protein, those nerve cells cannot properly function. They eventually die, leading to debilitating and sometimes fatal muscle weakness.

SMA is an autosomal recessive disorder, meaning the individual affected by SMA has inherited two copies of a non-working gene - one copy from each parent, or "carrier".

Carriers are individuals who do not have SMA, but who have one faulty copy and one functioning copy of SMN1. Approximately one in fifty people is a genetic carrier for SMA. Many times, carriers do not know until they have a child born to the disease.

When two carriers have a child, there is a 25 percent chance that the child will be unaffected, a 50 percent chance that the child will also be a carrier, and a 25 percent chance that the child will have SMA. This risk is the same for each pregnancy.

Most healthcare providers offer a genetic carrier screening either in the first trimester of pregnancy, or more lately they are initiating the testing as routine preconception care. This screening consists of simple blood work. Depending on those results, it's then determined whether the partner should also be tested. Remember, these autosomal recessive disorders require both parents to be carriers for a child to be at risk for inheritance.

I touched on the confusion surrounding my pregnancy with Hank. This head scratching all stemmed from that overlooked standard carrier screening in my first trimester. Now, after having Hank and being acutely aware of this information, we had to decide what it would mean for our future hopes for a family.

I didn't want to roll the dice of having another child affected with SMA. Even though the percentage possibility was 25 percent, it wasn't small enough. I made an appointment to start IVF in the months following Hank's death. As far as timing, what I can say is that the hope of having a piece of him back one day was what kept me going, so I didn't want to stall and let the pain sit, for fear I'd never try again.

In my case I wouldn't be doing standard IVF, I would be doing PGT-M: preimplantation genetic testing for monogenic/single gene defects. PGT-M is a genetic test that is performed on an IVF embryo (prior to transfer) that identifies the presence of a specific genetic mutation. This is the process for people in instances exactly like ours, who are carriers for a known disorder and want to ensure the embryos - and, in turn, children - will not be affected.

I listened to what the process would entail, and already drowning in grief, I honestly couldn't endure the daunting road ahead. We decided not to pursue IVF at the time, and we hoped the odds would be in our favor. After all, statistically we had a 75 percent chance of a healthy baby, and surely after the horror we just went through, we would get a win.

Well, that eleven week missed miscarriage that occurred after we lost Hank turned out to be another boy, and his diagnosis was identical (type 0/1 SMA). In early stages of a pregnancy there's typically no definite reasoning to put behind a miscarriage, but this was very likely the cause. To sidebar here, there are four classifications of SMA: types 0/1, 2, 3, 4. The classification depends on the number of backup gene copies a person has. Having more copies of SMN2 - the backup gene, is associated with less-severe symptoms and later onset. Type 0/1 is the most severe, presenting in infancy. Type 0/1 SMA is very rare and happens in only about 1 percent of *all* SMA cases, (a statistic I learned much later on). Despite this information of another diagnosis of SMA type 0/1, it was communicated we had simply gotten unlucky again.

We decided now was the time to see the PGT-M process through. There had been too much confusion and loss. Being pregnant in itself had become difficult enough with the anxiety it brought, and I couldn't handle any more uncertainty. I was confident with the decision and was glad to move forward.

After my first consultation appointment, I found out I was pregnant naturally. We weren't entirely surprised, as we both thought if it happened in this short interim, that it would be fate and we would be blessed with a healthy baby...*right?!* Yes, I was nervous, obviously; but when I saw those two lines again, I truly felt that this was it. It *had* to be. To put it mathematically, even though the chances for SMA in every pregnancy is 25 percent, hitting that outcome three times (maybe four) in a row is a probability of 0.4 percent.

At nine weeks I went to the ER with bleeding. I was miscarrying again. I spoke with the doctor on call and vented my frustrations, telling her there was no possible way someone could be this unfortunate. She listened, but she also backed up the notion that I had been given by numerous doctors previously, which was that these things just happen, and unfortunately, I kept pulling the short straw.

As you can imagine, I was now officially done with attempts of getting pregnant on our own again, so I resumed the PGT-M process. We had truly exhausted all efforts via the natural route, and it was time to make a hard turn. It was difficult for me to accept that I had picked the wrong fork in the road. I felt these losses added so much unnecessary suffering - and, more importantly, time wasted on top of what had already been such a difficult journey.

When the tissue analysis came back from the last miscarriage a few weeks later, it was discovered that this baby was a girl, and she carried an extra chromosome. Extra chromosomes are the most common reasons for miscarriages. When pushed for more information on this, again I was told it's completely spontaneous, and just happens when egg meets sperm. I understood in theory that this wasn't the craziest thing to happen. Miscarriages occur often. But it felt like a strange addition to an already bizarre sequence of events.

By happenstance of looking, I found out that the extra chromosome was an extra fifth chromosome, to be exact. Well, remember, when I said SMA is a mutation in the survival motor neuron gene? Which chromosome does that survival motor neuron gene live on? You guessed it: the fifth.

I was the one who brought this exact finding to the genetic lab that was responsible for making the customized genetic testing for our embryos. I have no medical background, but this coincidence seemed *too* ironic to not mean more. And, yet again, I was met with the reassurance that there was no correlation between that last miscarriage and our specific genetics.

During this exact time, I was asked to enroll in a clinical study for recurrent pregnancy loss through my hospital. Considering how many doctors and appointments I already had on the books, I wasn't exactly ready to sign up for anything time consuming. However, if the study was convenient, I was happy to do it. I figured maybe the oversights that happened to me could one day be avoided with more information. I was confused about how I could be useful in this study - all my losses had known causes, there didn't seem to be much more to unveil. I brought up the reasoning for my involvement to one of the research assistants, and within days I was in front of the study director, who (thankfully) looked over my chart with an eagle eye and was able to piece together what so many doctors before her couldn't.

She theorized that one of our fifth chromosomes have an additional mutation, break, or rearrangement beyond SMA. After months of waiting, the trial results concluded that although my husband is a "typical" carrier, I am not. I am missing additional genes on that fifth chromosome. Where most people have four SMN genes – two SMN1 and two SMN2, Spinal Muscular Atrophy carriers have three, (one SMN1 and two SMN2) whereas I only have one SMN1 gene altogether.

Instead of our children inheriting the disease 25 percent of the time, these missing pieces is recalculating the statistics to 50 percent, and resulting in this very severe case every time those odds hit. As to why they've hit every pregnancy? I likely have a random pre-disposition to pass the chromosome with 0 copies of the gene.

This revelation should have come with disappointment, but instead it came with clarity. I was appreciative that for the first time in this tumultuous journey it seemed like there was an understanding of the situation. Instead of looks of pity from doctors, I finally received some real, useful information. I finally met the beast I was fighting instead of having to swing in the dark.

I don't share these missteps as a knock on doctors, because I feel most of them did the best they could, with the information they had, or were taught in their respective fields. I share the missteps because, however incredibly rare my case may seem, both genetic disorders and medical oversight are not.

Genetics are complex; that's an understatement. I compare them to the galaxy, vast and often unknown. Some disorders are familiar stars that we know to look for; but many others, being as uncommon or unknown, don't have that recognition. It isn't until they are discovered or diagnosed that these rare disorders get brought to light.

When it comes to fertility and family planning, carrier screening is important. Doing research and questioning your medical care plan is important. Advocating for yourself is *very* important. It's difficult, as it's unknown territory for most, but when something seems off, dig deeper, ask questions, and be an advocate for yourself.

What does this mean for our future family? It would be a pleasure to end this story on the note of having a baby earth side with me, but this doesn't tie up in a neat little bow. It has loose ends. To save you from a complete headache of continued medical jargon- it's a long, twisty road, and it may, or may not work.

But that doesn't mean it isn't a happy one. My story is very much still being written, just like yours – and that's the point, isn't it? I can't wait for the trench in my heart to be somewhat filled with another child. Not a replacement, just like no one will replace the person you lost. We have to learn to enjoy life as it is. We have to find the beauty in what's left. We don't have time to wait to start living again.

In this I hope you've found a new friend, some comfort, and real advice to help guide you into the next chapter of life - and the strength to handle whatever it may, or may not bring.

I meant it when I said it - if you need someone, please reach out.
All inquires can be sent to: **fmn.shelby@gmail.com**

DEDICATION

Hank Ryan Michalek

I can say with certainty that you taught me more about life and love in those nine days than anyone or anything had in the thirty years before.

Whatever I make of this life, I will always first and foremost be your mom.

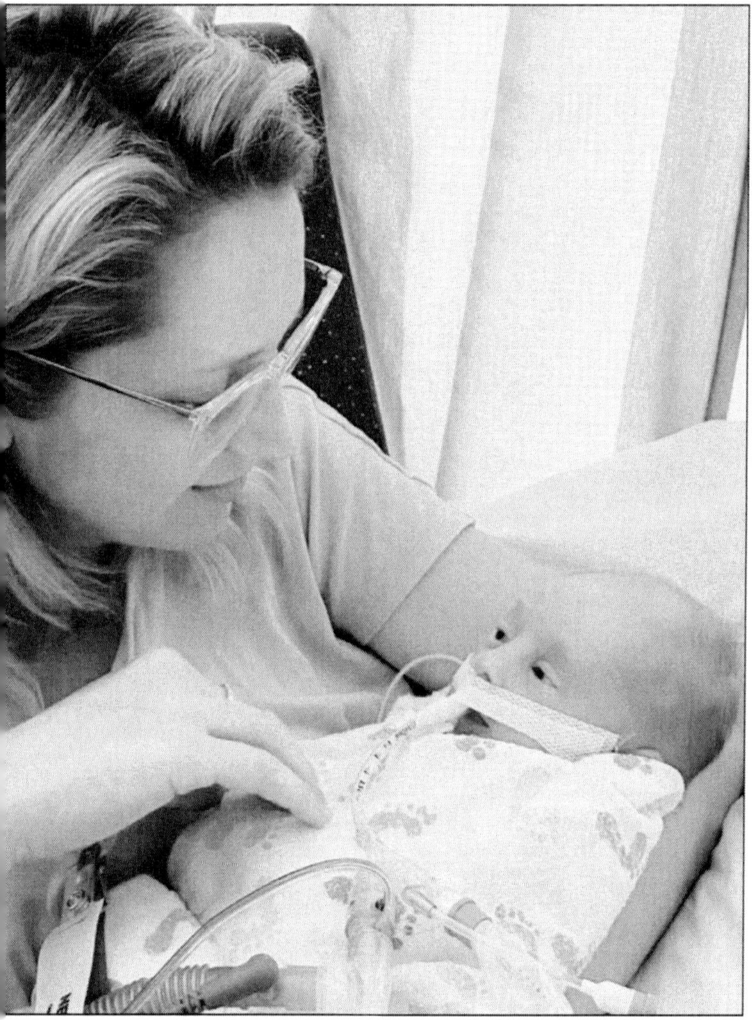

Made in United States
North Haven, CT
18 March 2024